Great Egret

Great Blue Heron

White Ibis

Wood Stork

Roseate Spoonbills

adult

immature

adult

immature

Herring Gull

Great Black-backed Gull

Western Gull

Heermann's Gull

Bonaparte's Gull

summer

Laughing Gull

winter

3

adult

immature

Ring-billed Gulls

Royal
Tern

Black
Skimmer

Least Tern

Shorebirds

Sanderlings

Western Sandpipers

winter

summer

Dunlins

Shorebirds

Clapper Rail

Willet

Long-billed Dowitcher

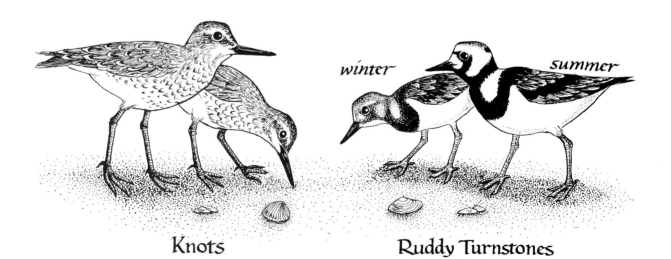

Knots

winter   summer

Ruddy Turnstones

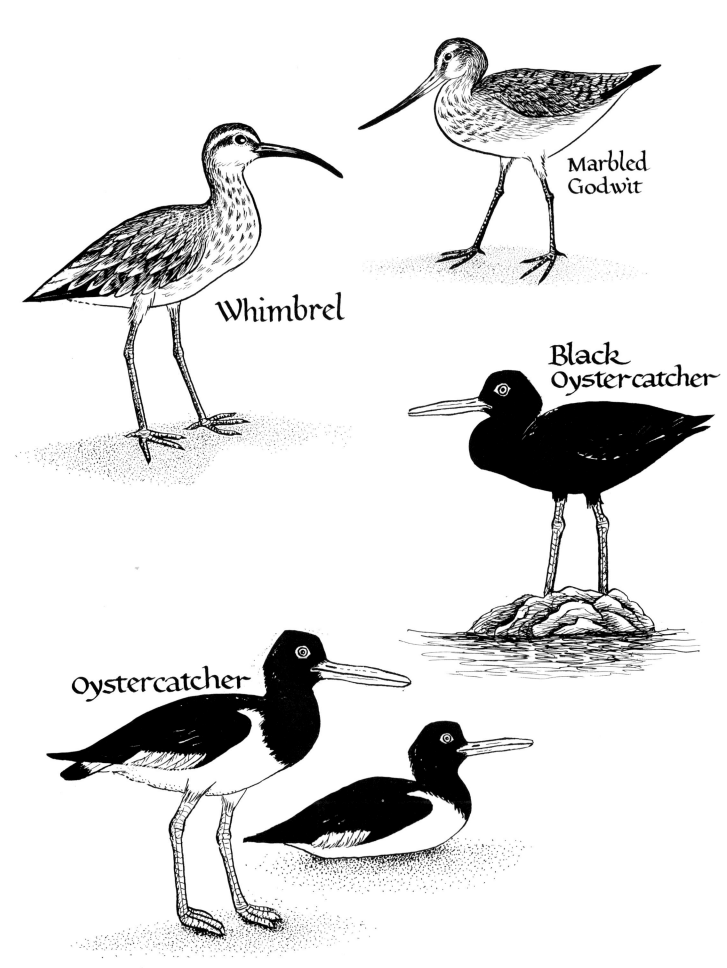

Marbled
Godwit

Whimbrel

Black
Oystercatcher

Oystercatcher

immature   adult

Brown Pelican

White Pelican

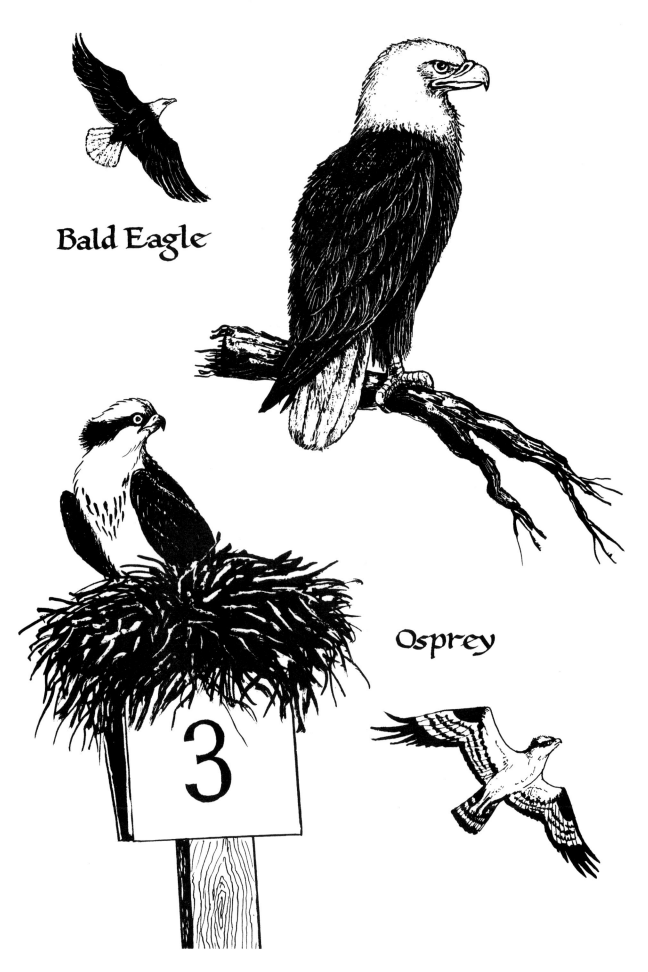

Bald Eagle

Osprey

3

Razorbill
Auk

Pigeon Guillemot

Puffin

Double-crested
Cormorant

Bufflehead   Surf Scoter   Scaup

Gannet

Frigatebird

male

female

male displaying on nest

13

Sea Otter

River
Otter

Sea Lion

bull

Harbor Seal

Bottlenose Dolphin

Florida Manatee

hatching
young

Loggerhead
Sea Turtle

Crabs

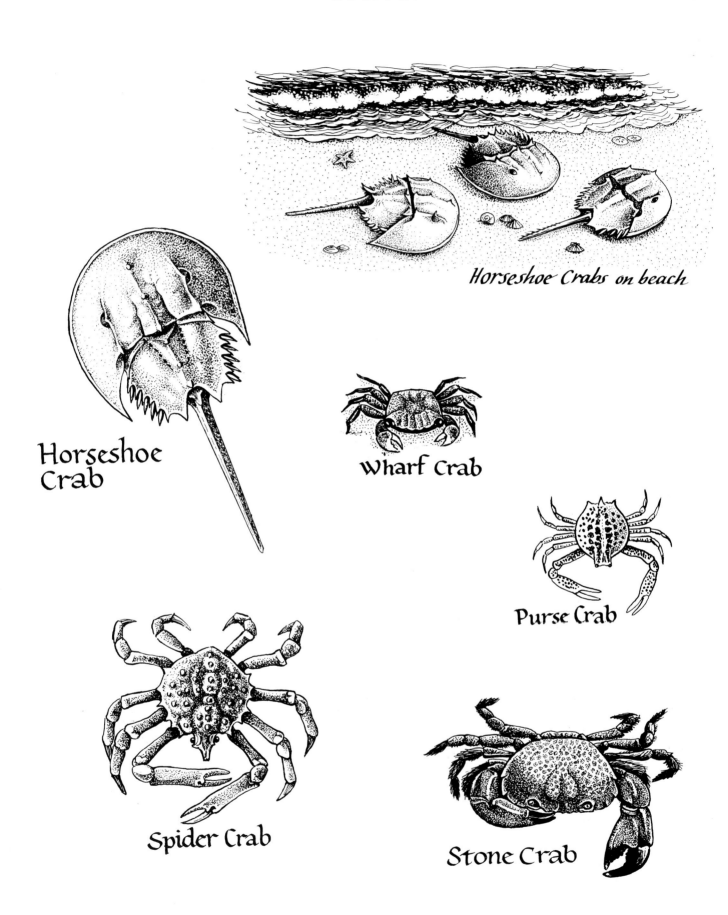

Horseshoe Crabs on beach

Horseshoe
Crab

Wharf Crab

Purse Crab

Spider Crab

Stone Crab

Lobster

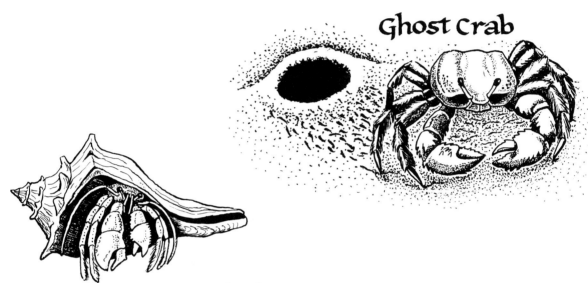

Ghost Crab

Hermit Crab in whelk shell

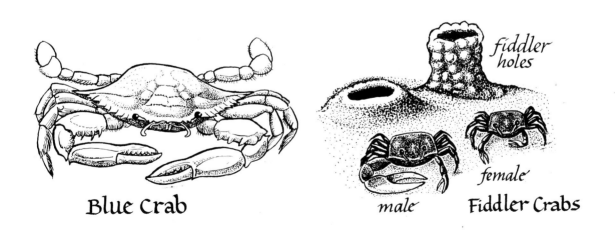

Blue Crab

fiddler holes

male *female* Fiddler Crabs

Acorn Barnacles

Goose Barnacles

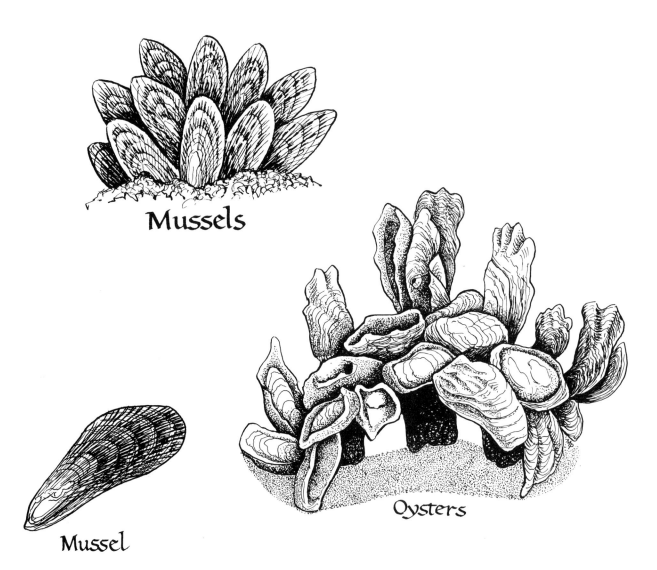

Mussels

Mussel

Oysters

Bivalves

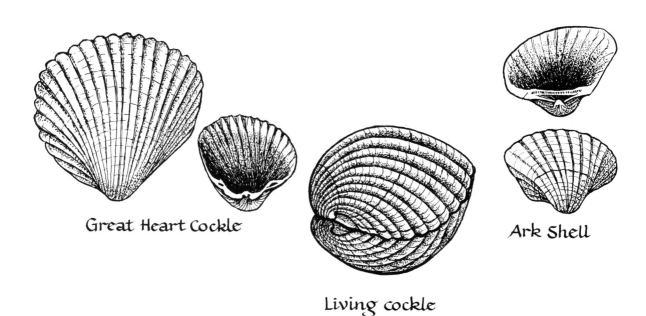

Great Heart Cockle

Living cockle

Ark Shell

Scallop

Prickly Cockle

Channeled Duck Clam

young clam

Quahog Clam

Geoduck

Bivalves

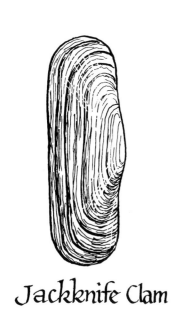

Jackknife Clam

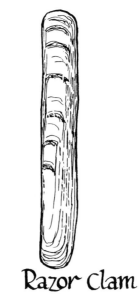

Razor Clam

Tellin

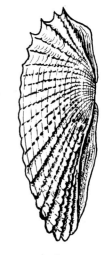

Angel wing

Geoduck

Surf Clam

Disk Clam

Coquina

Dwarf Surf Clam

Bittersweet Clam

Cat's Paw

Jewel box

Snails

Moon Snail

Olive Snail

Baby's ear

Slipper Shell

Oyster drill   Auger

Top Shell

Periwinkle

Nutmeg

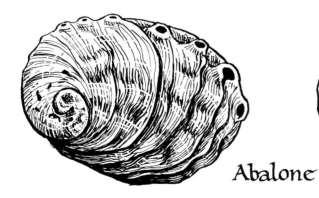

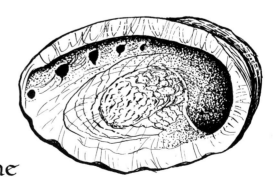

Abalone

Channeled Whelk

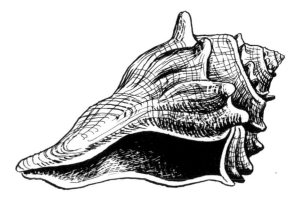

Knobbed Whelk

Fig *or* Pear Whelk

whelk egg case

living whelk

Tulip shell

Lightning Whelk

Fighting Conch

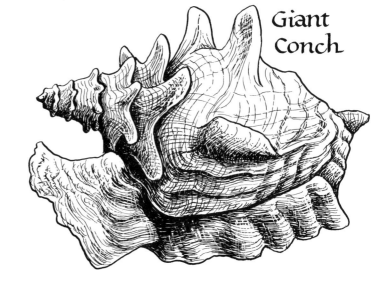

Giant Conch

Echinoderms

Common Sea Star

tube feet

Slender Sea Star

Sea Bat

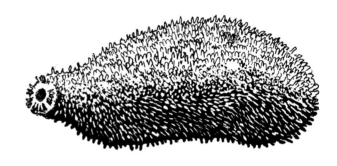

Sea Cucumber

Keyhole Urchin
or Sand dollar

Urchin test

Living Sea Urchin

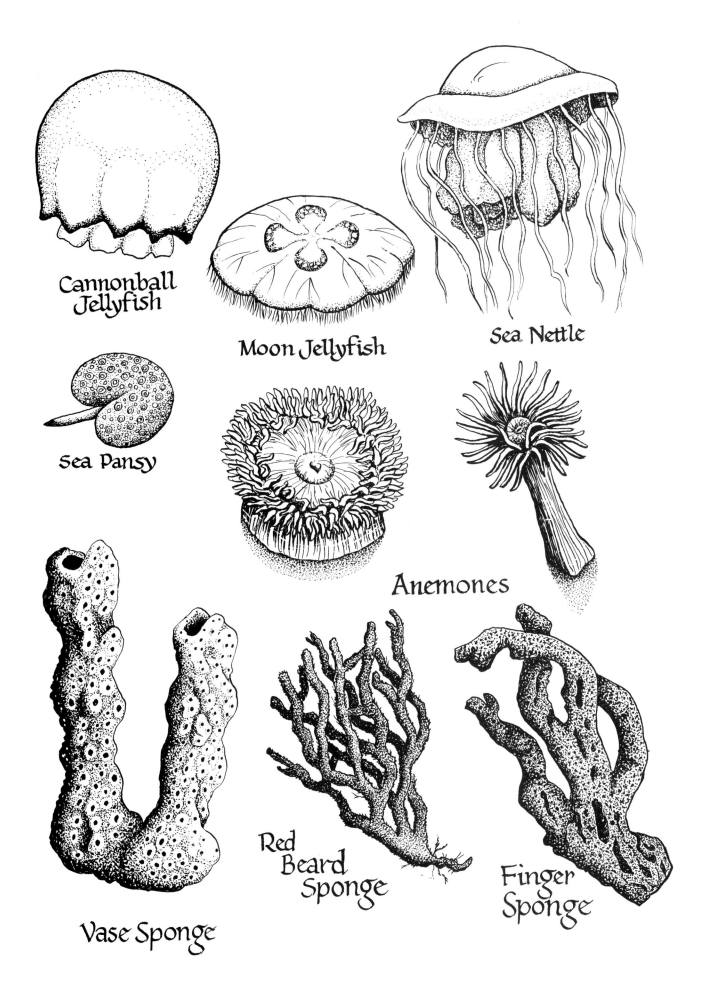

Cannonball
Jellyfish

Moon Jellyfish

Sea Nettle

Sea Pansy

Anemones

Vase Sponge

Red
Beard
Sponge

Finger
Sponge

26

The Dunes

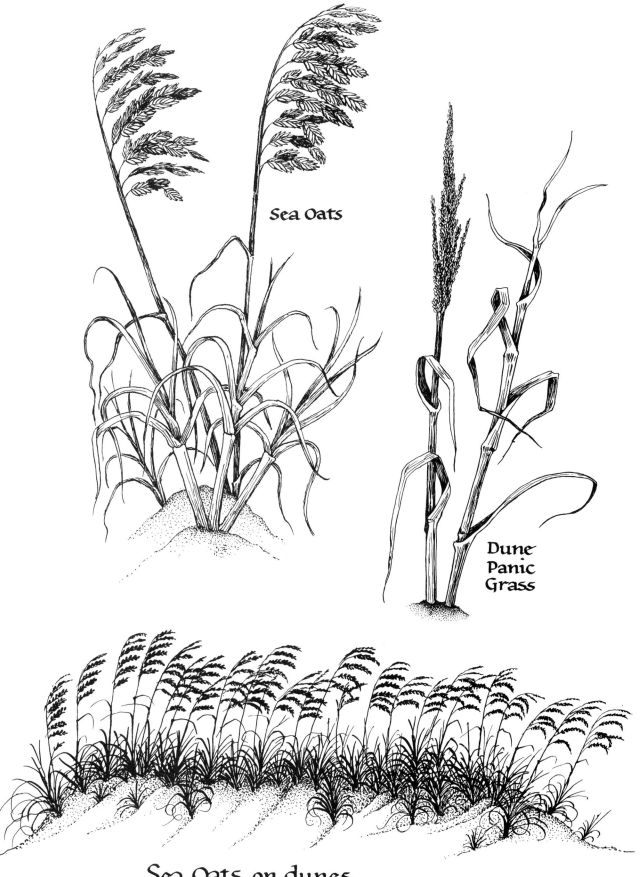

Sea Oats

Dune Panic Grass

Sea Oats on dunes

Red Cedar

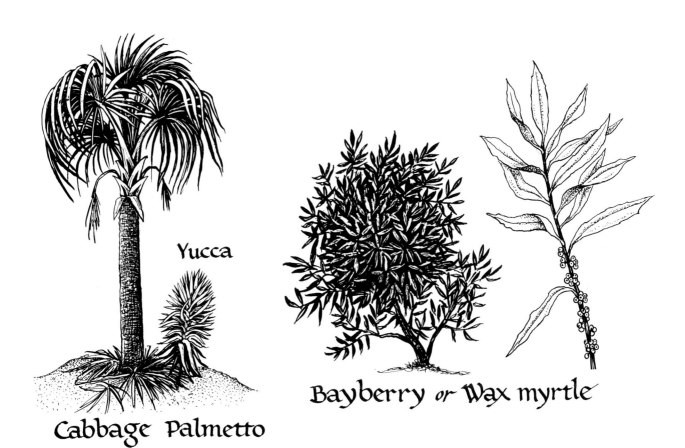

Yucca

Cabbage Palmetto

Bayberry *or* Wax myrtle

28

windblown oaks on dunes

Red Mangrove

Dune Plants

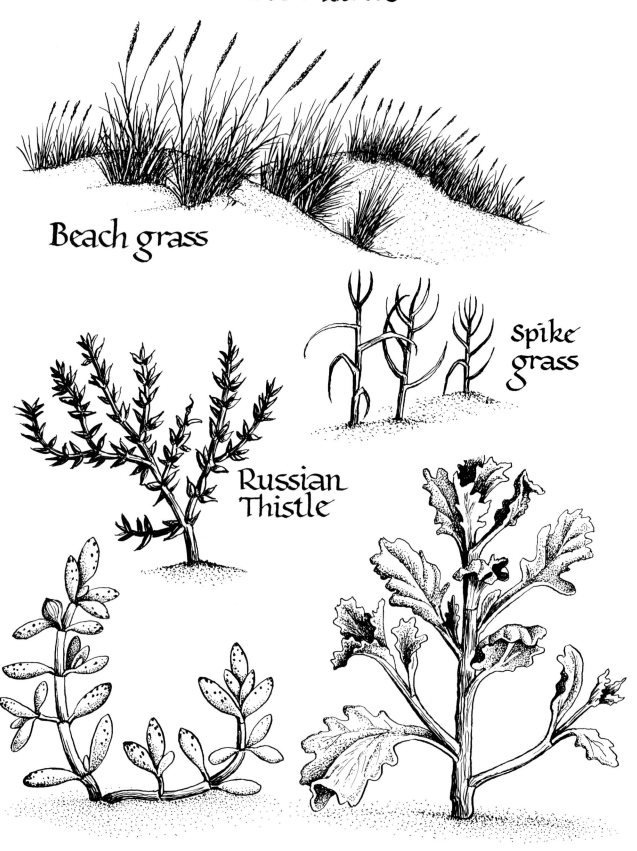

Beach grass

spike grass

Russian Thistle

Seaside Purslane

Sea Rocket

Dune Plants

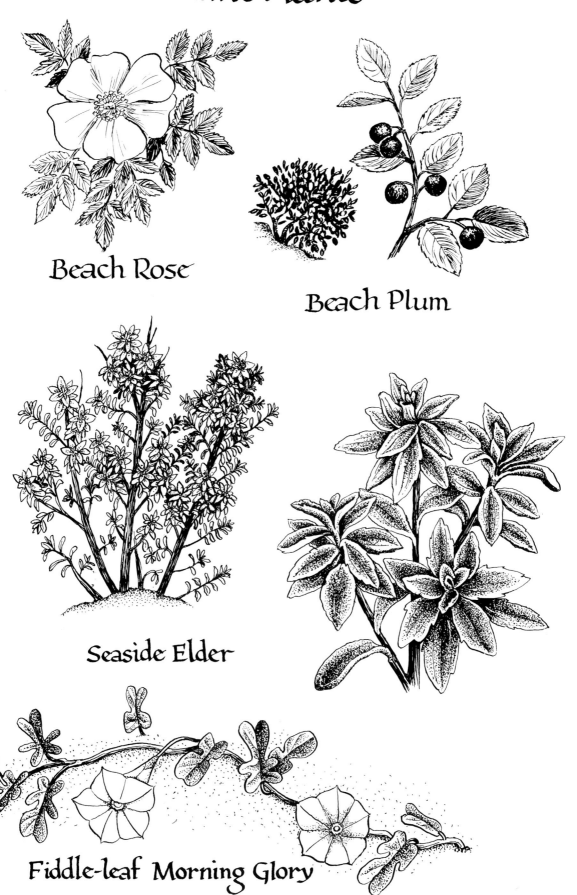

Beach Rose

Beach Plum

Seaside Elder

Fiddle-leaf Morning Glory

31

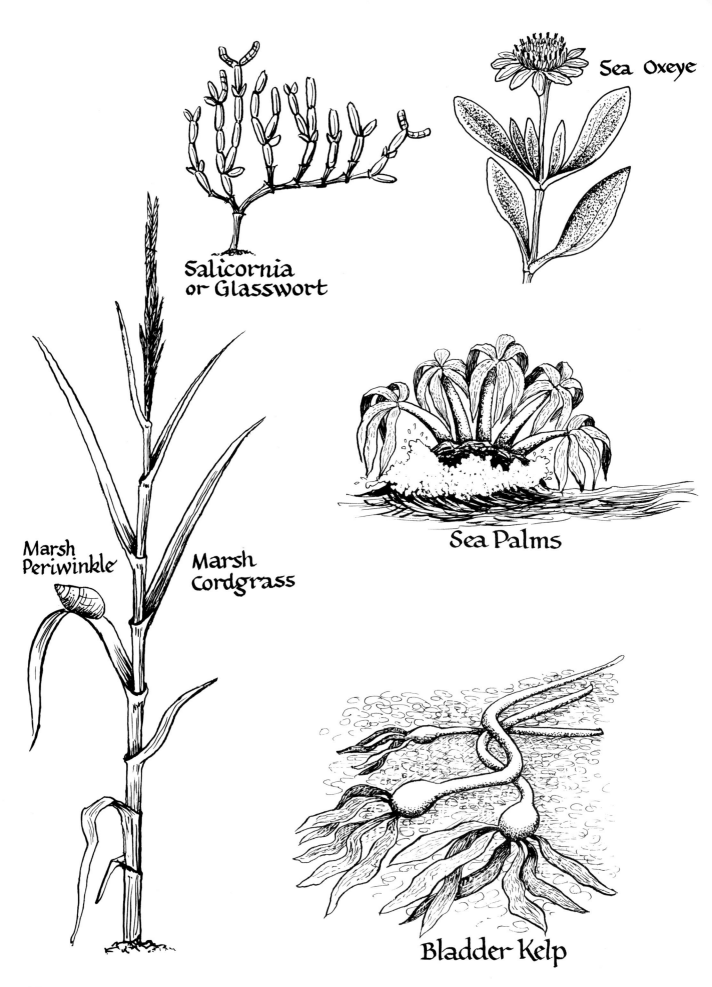

Salicornia
or Glasswort

Sea Oxeye

Sea Palms

Marsh
Periwinkle

Marsh
Cordgrass

Bladder Kelp